MW00857197

BACHELORETTE

BY LESLYE HEADLAND

DRAMATISTS
PLAY SERVICE
INC.

BACHELORETTE
Copyright © 2011, Leslye Headland

All Rights Reserved

SPECIAL NOTE

Anyone receiving permission to produce BACHELORETTE is required to give credit to the Author as sole and exclusive Author of the Play on the title page of all programs distributed in connection with performances of the Play and in all instances in which the title of the Play appears for purposes of advertising, publicizing or otherwise exploiting the Play and/or a production thereof. The name of the Author must appear on a separate line, in which no other name appears, immediately beneath the title and in size of type equal to 50% of the size of the largest, most prominent letter used for the title of the Play. No person, firm or entity may receive credit larger or more prominent than that accorded the Author. The following acknowledgments must appear on the title page in all programs distributed in connection with performances of the Play:

Produced by Second Stage Theatre, New York, 2010
Carole Rothman, Artistic Director

World premiere production presented by IAMA Theatre, January 2008.

SPECIAL NOTE ON SONGS AND RECORDINGS

Dramatists Play Service, Inc. neither holds the rights to nor grants permission to use any songs or recordings mentioned in the Play. Permission for performances of copyrighted songs, arrangements or recordings mentioned in this Play is not included in our license agreement. The permission of the copyright owner(s) must be obtained for any such use. For any songs and/or recordings mentioned in the Play, other songs, arrangements, or recordings may be substituted provided permission from the copyright owner(s) of such songs, arrangements or recordings is obtained; or songs, arrangements or recordings in the public domain may be substituted.

For my best friend, Melissa

BACHELORETTE was presented by IAMA Theatre Company at the Working Stage Theater in Los Angeles, California, opening on January 26, 2008. It was directed by Leslye Headland; the set design was by Whitney Whetstone; the lighting design was by CJ Longhammer; the costume design was by Josie Hamilton; and the sound design was by Annie McVey. The cast was as follows:

GENA	Melissa Stephens
KATIE	Louise Munson
REGAN	Laila Ayad
JEFF	Brandon Scott
JOE	Adam Shapiro
BECKY	Stefanie Black

BACHELORETTE was presented by Second Stage Theatre at the McGinn/Cazale Theatre in New York City, opening on July 26, 2010. It was directed by Trip Cullman; the set design was by Andromache Chalfant; the costume design was by Emily Rebholz; the lighting design was by Ben Stanton; and the sound design was by Jill BC Du Boff. The cast was as follows:

GENA	Katherine Waterston
KATIE	Celia Keenan-Bolger
REGAN	Tracee Chimo
JEFF	Eddie Kaye Thomas
JOE	Fran Kranz
BECKY	Carmen M. Herlihy

CHARACTERS

GENA, late twenties

KATIE, late twenties

REGAN, late twenties

JEFF, late twenties

JOE, late twenties

BECKY, late twenties

PLACE

An expensive hotel room, New York City.

TIME

The present.

"There is nothing like puking with somebody to make you into old friends."

—Sylvia Plath,
The Bell Jar

BACHELORETTE

Scene One

Two girls enter an expensive hotel suite.

There is a plush couch, a coffee table, two or three chairs, a desk, a large wall mirror and three doors, leading to a bedroom, bathroom and closet. The suite is decorated with many floral arrangements. There are many gifts wrapped in white wrapping paper.

The girls, both a bit drunk, stare in awe for a moment. They do not move.

Gena (pronounced "JEH-nuh") is a force to be reckoned with even in her dazed, intoxicated state. She is perhaps dressed a little boyishly, but she's always the sexiest woman in the room. Her alternately commanding then compassionate personality recalls a headstrong fifth grader.

Katie is a true beauty. Her dress is way too short considering her absurd physicality. Katie is all elbows and knees. She has a child-like unawareness of her sexuality. Her looks and wit have been dulled by years of binge drinking but her naïveté and smile are hard to resist.

Having sufficiently taken in their surroundings, they burst into laughter.

GENA. What —
KATIE. What the fuck?!

GENA. Are you kidding me?

KATIE. You. Are. Kidding! ME. *(Katie bolts into the room. Immediately jumps on the couch.)*

GENA. Don't break anything!

KATIE. Holy crap! *(Gena lights up a cigarette. Leaves the door to the suite ajar.)* Dude! Jump! On! This couch!

GENA. Dude. Chill! *(Katie falls off the couch and stumbles into the bathroom, offstage. Gena ignores her and wanders. She looks for something to ash in. She bumps into one of the floral arrangements. Gesturing to all the flowers.)* Fucking hell ... who died? You know?

KATIE. *(Offstage.)* Gena. You will not. BELIEVE what's in the bathroom. Come in here! *(Gena goes into the bedroom, gesturing to the bed as she enters.)*

GENA. *(Offstage.)* Her final resting place!

KATIE. *(Offstage.)* Come in here!

GENA. *(Offstage.)* Why? Are you doing coke?

KATIE. *(Offstage.)* What?! What ... *(Katie reenters, holding a bottle of expensive champagne.)* Oh my god. Where's the coke? *(Gena reenters. She is briefly unsure of where the coke might be. Then she remembers and pats her pocket.)*

GENA. I have it.

KATIE. You're like a guardian angel.

GENA. Katie ... um — what are you holding?

KATIE. *(A bit mystified.)* It's more alcohol.

GENA. THANK GOD!

KATIE. Do you know how to open this kind of —

GENA. Give it here, darling.

KATIE. — kind of device. *(Smiles.)* Can you smoke in here?

GENA. Nope.

KATIE. You smoke everywhere. *(Katie exits to the bathroom again. From offstage.)* Oh my god! That's what I was going to tell you.

GENA. What! KATIE! WHAT?! *(Katie reenters with another bottle of champagne and an ashtray for Gena.)*

KATIE. Hey, dude. Don't yell at me. I'm not the one getting married, okay?

GENA. My apologies.

KATIE. I was gonna saaaaaaaaaaay that there's like fifteen bottles of this shit *chilling* in the *bathtub!*

GENA. Fuuuuuck.

KATIE. Oh my god, I know. It's like so crazy! This is going to be the BEST night EVER! WOODSTOCK! *(Katie jumps on the couch.)* WOODSTOCK! MILLIONS OF PEOPLE! *(Breathes like throngs of people cheering.)* And Jimi Hendrix is like — *(Katie utilizes her champagne bottle like a guitar. She reenacts Jimi Hendrix playing "The Star-Spangled Banner," vocalizing the riff. Gena lights her lighter and waves it like she's at a concert. Affirming Gena.)* Totally! *(Katie continues her reenactment. Then she suddenly and violently sticks her middle finger up at the imaginary throngs of people.)* FUCK YOU! FUCK YOU BABYBOOMING PIECES OF SHIT! Jimi Hendrix ... If he really meant it ... if he REALLY REALLY meant it. He would have killed himself. I don't ... mean like snorting some bad shit ... Going out by accident, right? I mean like putting the barrel of shotgun in his mouth ... looking at a picture of his baby girl ... BAM! Pull the trigger.

GENA. Kurt Cobain.

KATIE. Jimi Hendrix wishes he was Kurt Cobain. Quick! Give me ... give me the lighter.

GENA. Absolutely not.

KATIE. Dude, I have to light my guitar on fire and like ... the "fuck-you" will be complete. Wait! If we got some heroin —

GENA. We don't do heroin.

KATIE. We should start. Call what's his —

GENA. *(Interrupting.)* I can't.

KATIE. Can we do some more coke?

GENA. We're rationing, man. Hard times.

KATIE. I'm depressed. I can't believe Pigface Fat Fatty FAT FUCK — *(Gena checks out the closet.)* What are you doing? What's in there?

GENA. The dress.

KATIE. *(Deflates.)* Jesus.

GENA. Yep. It's really happening.

KATIE. What does it look like?

GENA. Expensive. *(Then ...)* Beautiful. A beautiful white garbage bag.

KATIE. I hate her.

GENA. You can't hate her.

KATIE. Fat people are so easy to hate though.

GENA. Fat people have enough going on.

KATIE. *(Holding up the bottle.)* Can you open this?

GENA. I've already got one. Thank you.

KATIE. Will you open yours then?

GENA. You know where you'll get married? In your parents' back-yard in Long Island. Or is it technically your backyard as well since you live with them?

KATIE. Who do you think I'll marry?

GENA. Someone appropriate. *(She pops open her champagne bottle. POP! Lots of foam.)*

KATIE. Yah-ee!! Do mine. Do mine! *(Gena takes Katie's bottle. She exposes the cork.)* I think you'll run off with a Russian novelist. And we'll never hear from you again. We'll be like "What happened to Gena?" And I'll be like *(Whispers.)* "Russian novelist."

GENA. I don't think Russian novelists exist anymore.

KATIE. Then you'll marry an Arab. *(POP! More bubbles. The girls switch bottles.)*

GENA. What should we drink to?

KATIE. Life?

GENA. Sure. *(They both chug.)* Wow.

KATIE. Fuck.

GENA. Wow. *(They chug again.)* Can we have one of those moments?

KATIE. Yes … I think we should.

GENA. I just wanna say … that I'm … really …

KATIE. Let's drink more first. *(They chug. Katie gags a little. Gena pats her on the back.)*

GENA. I have …

KATIE. What?

GENA. I've no idea. I haven't been this fucked up since graduation.

KATIE. That was, like, a whole week of vomiting.

GENA. You were vomiting.

KATIE. Yeah, but you were like … crying and listening to Mozart.

GENA. *(Sighs.)* Yeah.

KATIE. *(Coughs.)* Can you believe how much Becky lucked out? She's marrying like the richest guy in the world. And he's good-looking.

GENA. Moderately good-looking.

KATIE. I wish I could kill myself, man.

GENA. Katie, stop it.

KATIE. Gena, seriously. I want to die and I can't bring myself to do it.

GENA. Woman. Chillax.

KATIE. Seriously. Did I ever tell you about the time —

GENA. *(Interrupting.)* Yes. *(Katie takes a swig of her bottle. Gena follows suit. Katie falls over.)*

KATIE. We were gonna have a moment.

GENA. Oh yeah.

KATIE. Let's have it.

GENA. *(After a moment.)* It's gone now.

KATIE. Let's do some coke and it'll come back.

GENA. If you do any more coke, someone's dick is gonna get sucked.

KATIE. Totally.

GENA. I think I was going to say something about —

KATIE. Becky?

GENA. — getting married

KATIE. To a moderately good-looking guy.

GENA. Who would've thought.

KATIE. And rich nonetheless. That word is awesome.

GENA. Nonetheless?

KATIE. Absolutely. I don't think I'm using it right.

GENA. Maybe Cal really loves her. Maybe he looks beyond, you know, "looks" and sees … She scares me Katie. Like I haven't seen her since the thing.

KATIE. What thing?

GENA. Remember … with me … her brother …

KATIE. *(Winces.)* Right.

GENA. Then out of the blue last minute she invites you and me to party the night before her wedding and has the decency to refrain from making us bridesmaids. Like that is classy and maybe that's what Cal likes about her.

KATIE. Are you trying to be positive?

GENA. I just think it's weird she invited us tonight. Like, what are we doing?

KATIE. Getting wasted.

GENA. Really, though. What are we doing here?

KATIE. Getting wasted. There's free booze. I'm excited.

GENA. I think the whole thing stinks. It's bugging me out. We shouldn't have come.

KATIE. We're bringing the party. She knows that's what we do. Right? I mean, what else would she be doing tonight? Rolling around in that bed wondering when that other shoe's gonna drop. Wondering if tomorrow at the altar Cal is gonna say "I do" and then add "but only if you lose sixty pounds."

13

GENA. Let's do some coke.

KATIE. Finally. *(Gena finds a clear surface to cut lines. She's a little stoned.)* We gotta do it before anyone else gets here. I don't want to share. *(Regan [pronounced "REE-guhn"] enters the suite. Regan is a queen bee if there ever was one. She has a fantastic body and a striking face. She is eerily perfect. If you look closely, it should be clear she was not born this way but has worked diligently to appear flawless. She has a penchant for meanness that no amount of beauty can hide. She rips off her expensive coat and tosses it to the floor. She kicks off her designer heels as if they were flip-flops. She throws her purse on the floor like it smells bad. She collapses in the nearest chair.)*

REGAN. Holy hell.

GENA. Where have you been?

REGAN. Are you guys doing some coke?

KATIE. Maybe.

REGAN. Thank god.

GENA. Where have you been?

REGAN. Clam-baking with some guys I met. There's only so much pot a girl can smoke before she gets to that point of not having any clue how she got somewhere. There's only so much Dave Matthews one girl can listen to before she considers throwing herself into oncoming traffic!

KATIE. Where are those guys?

REGAN. Trying to find a parking space.

GENA. Are they coming up?

REGAN. I wasn't sure if Becky would be cool with it. I'm gonna text them.

GENA. Where is Becky? I thought she was supposed to meet us here.

REGAN. Probably eating somewhere. *(Re: champagne.)* Where did you get that?

KATIE. There's like bottles and bottles chilling in the BATHTUB.

REGAN. Rich fiancées! If only we each had one of our own. *(Regan exits to the bathroom. Gena does a line of coke and passes a rolled-up bill to Katie, who follows suit. They snort lines throughout the following.)*

GENA. Are those guys cute?

REGAN. *(Offstage.)* They're repulsive. I was just excited about the pot. I haven't smoked since I was five.

KATIE. You got stoned when you were five?

GENA. Regan? What's the deal? Cuz I was gonna —

REGAN. *(Reentering with her own bottle.)* Do you have a date or something?

GENA. I don't want to dick around.

REGAN. Who's dicking around?

GENA. Why did you tell those guys they could come up here?

KATIE. Why not?

GENA. Because, Katie, this isn't our hotel room. And you don't realize this 'cause you like to check out early but usually Regan's schemes have this fantastic way of unraveling. Becky's supposed to meet us here and I —

REGAN. Don't worry about Becky. I'll take care of her.

GENA. I just wanna see this bitch. Throw some rice at her or whatever and get this shit over with.

KATIE. *(To Regan.)* You going to the … the thing tomorrow?

REGAN. What thing?

GENA. The wedding. It's tomorrow, right?

REGAN. Yeah. *(Points to herself.)* Maid of honor.

KATIE. How did you manage that?

REGAN. Someone had to fulfill best friend duties after Becky dropped Gena.

KATIE. 'Cause of the thing? With her brother?

REGAN. *(Nods, to Gena.)* She read me the email she sent you. Brutally epic.

GENA. Who gets married in a hotel?

KATIE. SO TACKY! Why weren't we invited to the wedding?

REGAN. Consider yourselves lucky. I had to go to the rehearsal dinner. I felt like Truman at Geneva.

KATIE. Is that bad?

GENA. SOMEBODY WENT TO AN IVY LEAGUE COLLEGE!

REGAN. Cal is a piece of work.

GENA. SOMEBODY GOT A SCHOLARSHIP TO PRINCE-TON!

REGAN. Cal bleaches his teeth. Can you imagine marrying a guy who has whiter teeth and less hair on his body than you?

GENA. Or is like half your body weight?

REGAN. It's one thing to like get engaged after three months of dating. I mean, I get it. But Becky's, like, never had a boyfriend.

KATIE. Never?

REGAN. I mean, she definitely didn't in high school. And I would've picked up on it if she had in college. We were CLOSE.

15

We threw up every meal together. Plus we all heard about it after she met Cal. "I met this guy … at work … "

GENA. I was surprised to hear that he works. I assumed people like that just swam in a pool of money all day.

REGAN. Kind of.

KATIE. What does he do again?

REGAN. Something with hedge funds. Becky was temping.

GENA. Swims in a pool of money all day. Becky was fishing the leaves out.

KATIE. I want a pool of money.

GENA. Don't worry, sweetie. You'll get it.

KATIE. I feel like the world is ending.

REGAN. It's not. It's just the first of us to get married.

GENA. I'm perfectly calm.

REGAN. I mean I was sure I was going to get married before her. But, you know what? We don't always get what we want. You know? I'm gonna break up with Frank.

GENA. Don't.

KATIE. You always SAY that.

REGAN. Why hasn't the idiot proposed to me? It's been three years and I'm like sitting around waiting for him to get through med school, so what … so he can dump me when he finds someone who will give him a blow job during football. Fuck that!

GENA. Dude. Just give him the blow job during football.

REGAN. No. I won't do that shit anymore. I know you've got to do it in the beginning. When we first got together, I sucked him off for the entire run time of *True Romance*.

KATIE. You went down on him during *True Romance*?

REGAN. The commentary.

KATIE. That is … gay!

REGAN. Blow jobs before dinner. Blow jobs after dinner. Blow jobs during the news, movies, sporting events. What the fuck? Is the quota ever filled?

GENA. You can't spoil them like that. They're like dogs.

KATIE. Or little children.

GENA. They'll get used to it and they'll expect it all the time.

REGAN. So you don't give head.

GENA. Excuse me! I go to town on those fuckers.

KATIE. Hell yeah!

GENA. You get me a dick and I'm like a fat kid eating cake!

REGAN. But it's a special occasion thing.

KATIE. Everything in moderation.

GENA. Speaking of which … *(Moves the coke away from Katie.)* Blow jobs are a delicate thing, my friend. You can't just go all out at the beginning of the relationship or affair or whatever. You gotta savor it which makes them savor it. You gotta make them feel like you're holding something back. You know?

REGAN. *(Pops the cork of her champagne.)* No. I don't.

GENA. Look. On a scale of one to ten, one being, like, you blow it kisses and ten being you're choking on vomit and semen. You gotta start out with fours and fives. You're just good enough that they feel like you know what you're doing but you're aloof … right? No enthusiasm. So he'll think, "Fine. I'll just fuck her." You start off with a ten and you've got nowhere to go. Why is he gonna spend any time fucking you when he just came all over your face? But if you start small … Then you build it up. Give him a six after a fight. Give an eight when he spends a lot of money on you.

KATIE. Eight is like … in the car. While he's driving.

GENA. On the way to your parents' house for Christmas.

KATIE. Then you can go back to fours and fives when you want him to do something like propose.

GENA. Exactly. He'll sense something's afoot.

KATIE. His dick alarm will go off.

GENA. And his dick alarm will go off. He'll ask, "What's wrong, baby?" when really he means …

KATIE. "Suck my dick harder."

GENA. This also cuts down on the passive-aggressive routine you've got going on.

REGAN. I'm not passive-aggressive.

KATIE. You are SO passive-aggressive. I know because I'm passive-aggressive and you make me look like the prom queen.

REGAN. You were the prom queen.

KATIE. Oh that's right. I was.

REGAN. But isn't rationing blow job potential passive-aggressive?

GENA. That's where you're wrong. Because this has nothing to do with emotions. This is science.

REGAN. It's Pavlovian.

KATIE. Pav —

GENA. Jesus Christ. *(Pushes coke in front of Katie … to Regan.)* You get what I'm saying?

REGAN. Yeah.

GENA. Good. Cuz I feel like my head is going to explode.

KATIE. I want to date someone who has a job.

REGAN. Can you believe I'm not getting married first? I mean I'm the one with the boyfriend. I'm hot! I, like, take care of myself.

GENA. It'll be okay, dude.

REGAN. I like exercise and eat like a normal person. I was totally the one who was going to get married first. Frank and I were gonna get married.

KATIE. Men suck.

GENA. No women suck. Men just taste bad.

REGAN. But, like, BECKY?! Why does this get to happen to Becky?

KATIE. Why does what get to happen?

REGAN. Like, marrying a Rockefeller and, like, before me and she's FAT. You know? She's fat!

GENA. She's not that fat.

KATIE. I mean ... she's not even like a real size.

GENA. According to who? The Gap?

KATIE. I don't work at the Gap anymore! Fuck off!

REGAN. I mean ... she's got a nice face.

KATIE. Don't do that.

REGAN. What?

KATIE. That "I just said something mean so I should say something nice" thing.

REGAN. Yeah. You're right. Fuck her. Becky's gonna be richer than any of us ever will be by three P.M. tomorrow.

GENA. This is about us. Not Becky.

KATIE. I just hope I'm married by thirty. If I'm not married by thirty, I will kill myself. I know you think I'm kidding but I'm not. I'll fucking put the barrel of a shotgun in my mouth.

GENA. Christ! Everyone needs to calm down.

KATIE. I'm totally calm. I just don't want to be thirty and still working in retail and NOT married. I'll fucking kill myself. I'll be like a bunion on the foot of the human race. I mean, you're complaining about Frank but at least you have those retarded kids to save.

REGAN. They're not retarded. They have cancer.

KATIE. Whatever. You know what I mean. You're interesting. You have a noble, like, crusade at the hospital and ... And at least you have a guy. At least you're getting cock. I don't even have prospective cock to passive-aggressively manipulate into marrying me.

GENA. Have you ever thought about getting pregnant?

REGAN. Are you crazy?

GENA. No. But I feel like I should've died ten minutes ago.

REGAN. I can't get fucking pregnant.

KATIE. Gena, that's a terrible thing to say.

GENA. I think we should slow down on the coke.

REGAN. I can't get pregnant. I can't just stop taking my contraception and get knocked up and just ASSUME the fucking bastard will stick around. That's like … like … Russian roulette …

KATIE. Except with human life.

REGAN. Yeah.

KATIE. HUMAN LIFE!

GENA. Is there some form of Russian roulette that DOESN'T involve risking human life?

REGAN. You know what I'm saying.

GENA. I miss Clyde.

REGAN. Gena!

GENA. I know I'll stop talking about it.

REGAN. You have to get over him.

GENA. I can't.

REGAN. It's been two years.

GENA. I can't help it. It's not even him I miss anymore. It's like this feeling he injected me with and I feel it all the time. Like the other day, I just stopped in the middle of Broadway and was looking downtown and the afternoon light was hitting the sides of the buildings in this way that just made my heart break. I almost called him.

REGAN. If you call him, I'll never speak to you again.

GENA. I texted him.

REGAN. Gena!

KATIE. Let's not fight. It's too awful on top of everything else. I don't want to go to work on Monday. I just can't stand going back there after like … being here … and like knowing what I'm missing.

GENA. You knew what you were missing before.

KATIE. *(Nearly crying.)* I know. I shouldn't read *US Weekly* anymore. It's too awful. I'm addicted. It's like porn for women. It's not fair. I can't stop. I can't stop. It's the clothes. I love looking at all the clothes.

REGAN. Let's not go into this.

GENA. Nobody wants to go to work on Monday. Even if they work with retarded kids.

REGAN. They have cancer.

KATIE. It's my own fault that I'm in credit card debt.

GENA. It's not your fault. You're a victim of the system. Those magazines and advertisers, they target people like you. Young white females with disposable incomes.

KATIE. And like, who said my income is disposable? You know? I need it.

REGAN. This is why Becky and Cal piss me off so much. You know? Why should SHE be the loophole?

GENA. I don't think she physically IS the loophole.

REGAN. Why does she get to never have to worry about money and do whatever she wants and like ... you know...? I hate her. I hope she dies. Let's set her dress on fire!

KATIE. Like Hendrix!

GENA. Katie's in a mood, Regan. Please don't encourage it.

KATIE. Oh my god. I would love you forever if you did that Regan.

REGAN. I mean, why did she invite us to party in this presidential suite or whatever it is. Like, what is this?

KATIE. Give me a lighter, Gena.

GENA. No. Regan, tell her to stop.

REGAN. I agree with her. Burn the bitch's dress.

GENA. No.

KATIE. Then the "fuck-you" will be complete!

REGAN. Fuck her, Gena. Becks doesn't deserve any of this.

GENA. You'll burn the whole place down. *(Katie dashes into the closet. Gena goes after her. Offstage, we hear them struggling to get to the dress first. Offstage.)* Ow!

KATIE. *(Offstage.)* No! My FACE!

GENA. *(Offstage.)* No tickling. I'm serious. STOP! *(During this offstage struggle, Regan picks up her designer bag and pulls out a prescription pill bottle. She picks out several pills, pops them into her mouth, and washes them down with champagne. Then she returns the bottle to her purse and throws it on the floor. Katie reenters, followed by Gena. She holds Becky's wedding dress. It's a masterpiece made comical by its size. Beat.)*

REGAN. Isn't it ridiculous?

GENA. It's retarded.

KATIE. Two people could fit in this!

REGAN. That dress. Almost broke her. It was altered four times before it actually fit her.

GENA. Let's put it back.

KATIE. I wanna try it on.

GENA. No!

REGAN. Knock yourself out. *(Katie slips it easily over her head. She swims in it. Doubles over with laughter.)*

GENA. You look like a *Carrie*-themed parade float.

KATIE. Two people could fit in this.

REGAN. Do you know how much that thing cost?

GENA. A semester of higher education?

REGAN. Practically. $15,000.

KATIE. Ugh! Gena, this thing could pay your rent for a year. And a half! Like two years. How many months does $800 go into …

GENA. I was told there'd be no math.

KATIE. How can Becky justify spending that on what is basically a tent made out of the skin of infants?

REGAN. She can afford it. She's paying for rent with her sex hole from this day forward.

KATIE. Someone get in with me. Let's take a picture, post it on Facebook and then tag Becky!

GENA. Dude! Take it off.

REGAN. That's a genius idea. I'll get in with you. Gena, take a picture!

GENA. Guys! Stop! *(They struggle. Regan manages to get one foot in. Gena pulls her. Riiiiiiiiiiiiiiiipppppppppp! All three girls freeze.)* That … just happened. Didn't it?

KATIE. Oh my god. *(Katie and Regan try to untangle themselves from the dress. Another … Riiiiiiiiiiiiiiiiiiiipppppppp!)*

GENA. Making it worse. Making it worse!

REGAN. Stop moving.

KATIE. Fuck. *(Regan trips away from the dress, now a pile on the floor.)*

REGAN. Okay. *(Katie steps gingerly out of the dress. Gena picks it up and surveys the damage.)*

GENA. Tell me this is okay. Tell me she can still wear this.

REGAN. *(Deadpan.)* It's okay. She can still wear it.

GENA. Dammit, Regan!

REGAN. Jesus. I don't know. *(She also surveys the damage. It doesn't look good.)*

GENA. What're we gonna do?

KATIE. We should hide it!

GENA. What?

KATIE. Tell her ... someone broke in and stole it! *(Katie begins to trash the hotel room.)*

GENA. *(Apoplectic.)* Regan!

REGAN. I guess ... you just tell her what happened?

GENA. Me? This wasn't my — *(Katie throws a glass vase onto the floor. CRASH!)* What the fuck —

REGAN. KATIE!

KATIE. We gotta make it look like the place was ransacked.

GENA. Regan. Please. Help me.

REGAN. This is probably a good time to let you know that Becky didn't want you two here tonight.

KATIE. What?

REGAN. Becky asked me not have you guys over here tonight. I thought "Screw her ... " But ...

KATIE. Why didn't she want us here?

REGAN. Because stuff like this happens when you two are around.

KATIE. Stuff like what? What happens? What exactly did she say?

REGAN. Becky said that I could use this room tonight 'cause she's staying in Cal's room. But that she really didn't want the whole "entourage" tonight.

KATIE. She said that?

REGAN. If she finds out you guys were here and ... that you did this ... Well, it's gonna be bad.

KATIE. I didn't do anything.

REGAN. You ripped her dress.

KATIE. But that wasn't my fault.

REGAN. Well ...

GENA. What're you saying? That you're gonna blame this on us?

KATIE. We were just playing around. *(To Regan.)* You stepped on it.

REGAN. It doesn't really matter. It's ripped now and you can blame me if it makes you feel better but ... I'm the only one out of the three of us who's supposed to be here.

GENA. If you think I'm lying under the fucking whatever for you on this one, Regan, you are out of your motherfucking mind.

REGAN. Well, someone needs to fix it and it's not gonna be me.

GENA. Why d'you have to make everyone else miserable just because Frank stopped fucking you when you turned twenty-seven.

REGAN. You're one to talk!

GENA. Go ahead rub fucking Clyde in my face again!

REGAN. Oh come on, Gena. I don't need this shit from you.

GENA. Get off my fucking dick. At least Clyde didn't string me along! At least he had the decency to tell me he didn't love me.

REGAN. Clyde ended with an abortion *I* had to drive you to. *(Beat.)*

GENA. Why did you just say that?

REGAN. Listen …

GENA. Why did you …

REGAN. It's nothing to be ashamed of, Gena.

GENA. I'm not ashamed.

REGAN. You are. But you shouldn't be. I just don't think it's fair for you to pull some sort of "holier than thou" routine with me when you're not being honest.

GENA. But I didn't … I wasn't.

REGAN. You were.

GENA. But that's … It's private.

REGAN. You can't expect me to keep secrets for you when I'm not even sure you're on my side.

GENA. I am.

REGAN. You weren't a second ago.

GENA. I am.

REGAN. Okay, then. *(Beat. No one moves.)*

KATIE. You guys had an abortion without me?

REGAN. *(Checks her phone.)* Those guys are texting me. They've probably circled the hotel like forty times. Shit. You should … maybe … start working on … *(Gestures to the dress.)*

GENA. Oh … yeah. I got this.

REGAN. You sure?

GENA. Yeah. I'll deal with it.

KATIE. Your nose is bleeding. *(Gena touches her nose. Blood drips from her nostrils.)*

GENA. Oh shit … Yeah. That happens. Sometimes.

REGAN. Are you okay?

GENA. Yeah. It doesn't hurt. It's just … You know … Life.

KATIE. What am I supposed to do?

REGAN. Go home. *(Regan gathers her things. As she finds Katie's belongings, she tosses them to Katie.)*

KATIE. I can't go home. The next train isn't until one fifteen. And it stops at, like, every stop. It'll take me three hours!

REGAN. We'll go see those guys. And they can drive you to Penn Station.

KATIE. I can't!

REGAN. Don't be such a baby. We'll smoke another bowl and you'll mellow out. It'll be fine. *(To Gena.)* Thanks.

GENA. Easier done than said. *(Katie and Regan exit. Gena takes a moment. She picks up the phone.)* Concierge, please. *(Waits.)* Hi, I need a tailor or something for a rip in a dress. How bad is it? Not that bad. It can be fixed. *(Blackout.)*

Scene Two

An hour later.

The hotel room is how we left it. Still a mess. The lights are on.

Noises. We hear the door open.

REGAN. *(Offstage.)* No! Leave the door open for the … other people. *(Regan stumbles in. She is much more high than she was before. Spacey. Slower. She kicks off shoes, tosses coat, throws purse. Just as she did before. Close behind her is Jeff, a good-looking guy who actually swaggers. He's practically wearing a suit. But it's not a suit. Jeff is self-assured with maybe a successful middle management job, probably graduated summa cum laude and definitely has fucked hookers.)* I don't wanna go through that whole ordeal again.

JEFF. You really sweet-talked that guy at the front desk.

REGAN. My idiot friend is the only one with the key. *(Shouting.)* Gena! *(To Jeff.)* I forgot to get it.

JEFF. And the coke.

REGAN. What?

JEFF. She's got the coke too.

REGAN. Did we already talk about this?

JEFF. Yes.

REGAN. Sorry. I'm really fucked up. I never smoke pot. It's so pedestrian.

JEFF. Don't be sorry. *(He touches her seductively. Regan lets him but hardly notices. She gets her cell phone and dials.)*

REGAN. Should've grabbed the coke. I'm about to fall asleep.

JEFF. Whose room is this?

REGAN. I gotta order some coffee or something. Before we smoke more. I just — *(Pause, then into her cell.)* Gena, where are you? Where's the ... um ... Becky's thing ... I need you ... to call me.

JEFF. *(Looking out the window.)* That's quite a view.

REGAN. What? Oh yeah. See! I told you.

JEFF. Whose room is this?

REGAN. Oh. It's this girl's. A friend. We used to live together in Park Slope. She's getting married here tomorrow. Downstairs. In some "Gold Room" or something. *(During the following, Regan goes to the land line and dials Room Service.)*

JEFF. Good for her.

REGAN. You probably don't go in for that sort of thing do you?

JEFF. Do you?

REGAN. Maid of honor.

JEFF. What do you do as the maid of honor?

REGAN. Nothing.

JEFF. So what's the point in having one?

REGAN. What the fuck does the "best man" do? *(Into the phone.)* Can I get like eight black coffees?

JEFF. I was the best man once.

REGAN. *(Into the phone.)* As soon as possible. Like immediately.

JEFF. For my friend Albert from Northwestern. We were in this fraternity.

REGAN. *(Into the phone.)* Yeah. A pot is fine. Whatever you ... usually do.

JEFF. That guy was crazy. Works for Mircosoft now.

REGAN. *(Into the phone.)* Yeah. One espresso then. And a pot.

JEFF. Knocked up his girlfriend. So they got married. Now they've got this baby and it's all they talk about. You're. Not. Even. Listening to me.

REGAN. I was. Mircosoft baby. Riveting. *(Joe enters. Slumped over him is a very very very wasted Katie. Joe is a variation of those easygoing stoner types that have become so fashionable to fuck now. Joe is in no way the fashionable version. More like the listens-to-jam-bands-and-John-Zorn version.)*

JOE. Thanks for waiting for us.

JEFF. Snooze you lose.

JOE. I had to park and I don't know if you've noticed but I've only got my right arm to work with here.

JEFF. It's not like you're left-handed. Did you bring the weed?

JOE. Yes.

JEFF. You wanna pack a bowl?

JOE. Can you just hang on a second?

JEFF. Why didn't you valet?

JOE. You have to pay for that.

REGAN. Just charge it to the room. I'll be right back. *(Regan exits to the bathroom. Joe sits Katie down in a chair. She goes in and out of consciousness. Joe gets his weed and bowl out. He packs it.)*

JOE. Whose room is this?

JEFF. Who cares?

JOE. I'm just making sure we're, like, allowed to be here.

JEFF. You worry all the time. Stop worrying.

JOE. I'm not worrying.

JEFF. This is so typical of you, Joe. Don't you get it? We just hit the proverbial jackpot. We are going to get laid tonight. Probably several times. In a five-star hotel. And you're worried. About what? Getting detention from the hall monitor. That girl in the bathroom was practically going to blow me in the car. Give me fifteen minutes. Another bowl. And I'll leave you alone with yours.

JOE. Mine's going to pass out. If she hasn't already.

JEFF. Well, she's hotter than mine so it all evens out.

JOE. I guess so.

JEFF. I know so. *(Regan reenters with two bottles of champagne.)*

REGAN. Greetings. I bring gifts.

JEFF. *(Taking one.)* Thank you.

JOE. *(Declining.)* I'm packing a bowl.

REGAN. *(Re: the weed.)* The more the merrier. *(When bowl is packed, Joe lights and smokes it. He, Jeff and Regan pass it around during the following dialogue.)*

JEFF. So what do you do?

REGAN. I work at a hospital. It's really boring.

JEFF. Doesn't sound boring.

REGAN. I'm boring when I talk about it.

JEFF. I don't think I would ever use the word "boring" to describe you.

REGAN. Right. Don't do that.

JEFF. I'm not doing anything.

REGAN. You're totally doing it.

JEFF. I'm genuinely interested in what you do for a living. Is that a crime?

REGAN. No.

JEFF. You're really on the offensive.

REGAN. I'm not. I don't mean … mean to be. I'm just stoned.

JEFF. Relax. We're in a beautiful place. Look! *(Indicates the view.)* Look at that! Central Park. All those people out there without anywhere to sleep tonight. And we're just floating above them. We're safe. You don't need that armor.

REGAN. Armor?

JEFF. That suit you put on every day. That shield of "fuck off" that protects you.

REGAN. I don't … have … a shield.

JEFF. We all do. Tonight is not yesterday. It's not tomorrow. It's right this second.

REGAN. What were we talking about?

JEFF. Your job.

REGAN. *(Prosaically stoned.)* Well … I'm not even a real doctor or anything. I mean, I will be someday. But right now I'm working with these sick kids. These kids who've been diagnosed with cancer and, you know, chemo when you're like twelve sucks. It sucks no matter what but like twelve sucks. Twelve sucks in general. Like you don't know … you just don't know. Cuz you're a guy. But like twelve. That's when it happens man … that's when it happens.

JEFF. When what happens?

REGAN. When you start to hate yourself.

JOE. Is your friend going to be okay?

REGAN. Who?

JOE. Um …

REGAN. KATIE! *(Katie lifts her head. Joe offers her the bowl. Katie leans toward it. Joe holds it for her and lights it so she can inhale without using her hands. She coughs.)*

KATIE. *(Leaning on Joe.)* Thanks. I'm fucked.

JOE. That's okay.

KATIE. I'm tired.

REGAN. You can't sleep.

JOE. Well, I think she's —

REGAN. KATIE! WAKE UP!

KATIE. *(To Regan.)* You didn't even say anything about my dress.

REGAN. No sleeping.

JEFF. Wait. I'm really interested in this hating yourself thing.

REGAN. What? Oh … Jeff, you wouldn't understand.

JEFF. Try me.

REGAN. It's a girl thing.

JEFF. Don't be like that.

REGAN. Fine. You start bleeding.

JEFF. Don't cop out.

REGAN. I can't … I can't talk to you about it.

JEFF. Why did you bring it up then?

REGAN. Because I'm wasted.

JEFF. I think you want to talk about it.

REGAN. You don't know what I want.

JEFF. I think you do. I think you want me to tell you not to hate yourself. That you're beautiful and that what you're doing with the kids is awesome. But that's not me. I'm not going to do that. I like to compliment a woman because I feel like it. Not because she needs attention.

REGAN. I don't NEED attention. I have a boyfriend. I get plenty of attention.

JEFF. Then why are you here. Why aren't you with him tonight?

REGAN. It's none of your business.

JEFF. I think you're unhappy and you have no reason to be and that makes you hate yourself.

REGAN. Let me guess. Psych major. Psych major with a lucrative advertising job.

JEFF. That's right. Belittle me. Is that what you do to your boyfriend? Does it work for him?

REGAN. Not really.

JEFF. Maybe you should change your tactics.

REGAN. There is nothing wrong with … with my relationship. And I don't care what you think anyway.

JEFF. Right. That's why you're so calm and unaffected by me. *(Regan glares at him.)* Oh. You're mad. You're so mad.

REGAN. I am not.

JEFF. You're so mad you can barely restrain yourself.

REGAN. I'm not mad.

JEFF. Fine. I'm glad you're in such a good mood. *(Katie hiccups a little. Joe pushes her hair back.)*

JOE. Are you gonna throw up? You want to go to the bathroom with me? *(Katie spits onto the floor.)*

KATIE. Ugh ...

JOE. Let's go to the bathroom. *(Joe briskly helps her to her feet. They exit to the bathroom.)*

JEFF. Your friend is pretty fucked up.

REGAN. She's a lightweight.

JEFF. You look beautiful right now.

REGAN. I thought you didn't give compliments.

JEFF. No. I said I only give compliments when I genuinely mean them.

REGAN. And I suppose this — *(Gestures at Jeff's persona.)* is genuine.

JEFF. Why don't you like me?

REGAN. I do.

JEFF. You have a funny way of showing it.

REGAN. This whole night's been a shitshow. I feel like Truman at Geneva.

JEFF. That doesn't make sense.

REGAN. What?

JEFF. You mean ... I think you mean Truman at Potsdam.

REGAN. What?

JEFF. Truman had just inherited the presidency due to the fact that Roosevelt died. He had to jet over to Berlin where he was dealing with Stalin and Churchill. He was completely inexperienced and had very little briefing, so I can see how you could make the analogy to your shitshow in that sense. The Geneva conferences are something else altogether. One in 1932 and I think Truman was running a hat shop at the time and another in the fifties after he ... like wasn't president anymore. So I think you mean Truman at Potsdam. *(Beat.)*

REGAN. Yeah. I mean, I'm wasted so I switched it or ... something.

JEFF. But it still doesn't really make sense because Truman had a trump card. He had the atomic bomb. So he was really in control the whole time.

REGAN. Well ...

JEFF. What's it like being wrong?

REGAN. It feels great.

JEFF. *(Touching her.)* Yeah?

REGAN. Mmmhmm.

JEFF. *(Slips his hand in her dress.)* You like that?

REGAN. Yeah …

JEFF. You need someone to tell you.

REGAN. Mmm.

JEFF. *(Groping her.)* Yeah?

REGAN. Tell me … *(Jeff buries his face in her neck.)* Tell me what?

JEFF. Just that you're wrong. That you're not as smart as you act. That you're really just a little girl. You just act like a bitch because that idiot lets you.

REGAN. Yes. *(Jeff slips his hand between her legs.)*

JEFF. You want someone to put you in your place.

REGAN. Where's that?

JEFF. Where do you want it? *(Joe blusters in from the bathroom. He barely acknowledges Jeff and Regan's position but does acknowledge it. He has some vomit on his shirt.)*

JOE. She's asking for her purse. Does anyone … like, know where it is? *(Jeff and Regan look at him coldly.)* It's probably in the car. *(Joe exits to the bathroom. Jeff attempts to move this into the bedroom.)*

JEFF. Let's go lie down.

REGAN. *(Softly.)* No. No.

JEFF. Come on. Let's lie down.

REGAN. I don't … I can't … have sex with you.

JEFF. We don't have to have sex.

REGAN. I'll get in trouble.

JEFF. I am not that guy. *(Touches under her skirt, groping softly.)* I just want to feel that. Right there. How you tremble like that? I just want to feel that. Can I do that?

REGAN. *(Enjoying it.)* Uunnhh …

JEFF. Look at you. That's beautiful. When I do this …

REGAN. Let's go. Come on … let's go. *(They exit to the bedroom. Joe reenters and goes straight to his weed. Katie reenters. Her face has been washed and her hair is a little wet. They sit together.)*

KATIE. I feel so much better.

JOE. Good.

KATIE. I really feel good now.

JOE. Good.

KATIE. Mmm-hmm.

JOE. I'm gonna smoke more, okay?

KATIE. Okay.

JOE. I just … don't want you to think I'm weird.

KATIE. *(Spacey.)* Nooooooo.

JOE. This girl who used to babysit me and my brothers when we were little smoked pot on our patio. And I lost all this respect for her. It looks weird when someone smokes by themselves.

KATIE. I don't think you're weird.

JOE. I'm gonna do it anyway. I don't know why I felt the need to point out how weird it is when I was gonna do it anyway.

KATIE. I'll do it with you.

JOE. You probably should take it easy, maybe.

KATIE. Thank you.

JOE. For what?

KATIE. For ... helping me.

JOE. *(Taking a hit.)* Oh yeah. Sure. You're really cool.

KATIE. You're cooler.

JOE. No. Everyone's been there.

KATIE. Where?

JOE. You know ... *(Gestures to the bathroom.)* It happens. You party too much ... Then you puke.

KATIE. Party too much. *(She nuzzles his shoulder, then leans on it. This makes it hard for Joe to smoke.)*

JOE. Yeah.

KATIE. Do you have a job?

JOE. Yep.

KATIE. Me, too.

JOE. Let's not talk about it.

KATIE. I work at a store. Where they sell clothes.

JOE. I hang wallpaper.

KATIE. That's amazing.

JOE. Yeah ... *(Pause.)* Hey. This bowl is done. I have to pack it again.

KATIE. Mmm-hmm.

JOE. I need to move my arm.

KATIE. I'm sorry. *(Moves away.)* I'm so retarded.

JOE. No. I'm sorry ... It's just ... I need to move it for a second ... then it's all yours. *(He packs the bowl. When he's done, he lights and smokes again.)* Is this your hotel room?

KATIE. It's Becky's.

JOE. Is she your friend or something?

KATIE. She's fat.

JOE. Oh.

KATIE. Do I look okay?

JOE. Yes.

KATIE. Even though I just threw up?

JOE. Yes.

KATIE. Do you smoke pot a lot?

JOE. Yes. I do. That girl. I was telling you about. She started smoking me out when I was like ... Smaller than I am now.

KATIE. I bet you were cute.

JOE. Not really.

KATIE. How old?

JOE. She was like sixteen. I guess. *(Pause.)* I'm not saying she like got me addicted or anything. I don't think pot is addictive. I think it's pretty natural. That was when I started and I never stopped. I guess. Just like it too much. *(Katie picks up an open champagne bottle. She chugs it.)* You might puke again if you do that.

KATIE. I don't think ... that's any of your business.

JOE. Whatever. *(She chugs again.)* Why do you drink so much?

KATIE. Why do you smoke even if no one else is?

JOE. Because ... I mean, I told you.

KATIE. I like when I can't bring the bottle to my mouth anymore.

JOE. Right.

KATIE. That hasn't happened yet.

JOE. I just don't think you want to puke again.

KATIE. I don't care.

JOE. Okay.

KATIE. I want to get to that point.

JOE. Where you can't lift the bottle to drink more?

KATIE. Yes.

JOE. Does that feel good?

KATIE. It's the best.

JOE. I can respect that.

KATIE. What?

JOE. I can respect wanting that. That feeling.

KATIE. Yeah?

JOE. Sure.

KATIE. I just threw up on you.

JOE. You think that hasn't happened to me?

KATIE. Well ...

JOE. One time I passed out on the toilet in my own shit.

KATIE. *(Laughs.)* I woke up naked next to a hamburger once.

JOE. *(Laughs.)* Awesome.

KATIE. I was like "I just fucked that hamburger."

JOE. I was tripping on 'shrooms this one time and I was convinced I was Satan. So I lit my friend's couch on fire. *(Katie laughs harder.)*

KATIE. When things get that bad, I feel like Marilyn Monroe.

JOE. I used to be obsessed with her. I read like every book on her ever. And the thing that I always thought was incredible was what … Like people … They think of a white skirt over a subway grate or a pink gown and diamonds. Blond hair. Everything she did to cover up who she really was. They don't think about her vomiting from too many pills or getting wasted and throwing her drink in Peter Lawford's face or something. That's what made her the greatest actor ever. And maybe she had to go that crazy in order to be the perfect woman. You know?

KATIE. I tried to cut my wrists open with a broken bottle. *(Beat.)*

JOE. Tonight?

KATIE. Probably a year ago.

JOE. Of course not tonight.

KATIE. I'm sorry.

JOE. No.

KATIE. I don't know —

JOE. No.

KATIE. — why I said that. I just …

JOE. *(Takes a hit.)* I went out drinking one night with my friend, Ethan. We'd been friends since, like, third grade. We got blasted. Stumbled back to my place and passed out in my bed. Lying side by side. He never woke up. He just never woke up. They said it was alcohol poisoning. But it turned out he had hepatitis too. So I don't know. He had started this whole heroin thing. Anyway … Maybe … there's something … he didn't look dead. You know? Even at the funeral, with the entire high school there, he just didn't look dead. It was like at any moment he was going to wake up and tell me I was a pussy for buying into this whole mourning and wearing black thing. I wanted to just get high. I felt like that was what he would've wanted. Not all this eulogizing and sober bullshit. But my parents … it was crappy. I had to pretend to be this person who was really concerned. That's not the right word. But I had to be this, like, adult or something. Why? You know? You can't just magically stop. Ethan fucking never woke up but it doesn't make me magically turn into someone who doesn't smoke or drink or get high or whatever. I resent that shit. Like the so-called "wake up" call. What the fuck? Ethan lucked out. When they put him in the ground, I knew he'd gotten away with it.

KATIE. Got away with what?

JOE. He never … he never had to grow up. I know that's fucked up. But I feel like whatever … it's one of those nights, right?

KATIE. *(Desperately.)* Yes!

JOE. I feel like you get it. Look at me. I'm twenty-nine and the only difference between me then and now. The only change in twelve years … is that I'm, like, taller. And it's not because I'm, like, some loser. It's because I saw everyone scurrying off from that grave. Like "Holy Shit! We better all grow up. We better not end up like Ethan fucking Parsons." And why? For what? *(Beat. Joe takes a hit. Katie stares at nothing.)*

KATIE. I can't believe … that I haven't blacked out yet. What time is it?

JOE. *(Checks his phone.)* Almost midnight.

KATIE. It's early. I love blacking out. It's like sleeping except … better.

JOE. Are you freaked out by my story?

KATIE. No.

JOE. I just think you're cool and I figured you … would, like, get it. I guess.

KATIE. I told you I tried to kill myself.

JOE. Lots of people try to kill themselves. Marilyn Monroe pretty much killed herself.

KATIE. Yeah.

JOE. You know who you remind me of?

KATIE. Your sister.

JOE. No. I don't have a sister.

KATIE. The prom queen.

JOE. Well … yeah a little.

KATIE. I was the prom queen. It was great. I was fucking awesome. I got to wear a crown and a dress from Neiman Marcus. And everyone hated me.

JOE. You're not that hateable.

KATIE. Everyone hated me. But you know what? It's better than being ignored, which is all anyone does to me now. You know what I hate the most about my job. When I say, "Can I help you?" And people just look at me like I'm a lighting fixture. I mean, even the people who have nothing but disdain for me don't piss me off as much as the people who think I'm part of the scenery. *(Drinks.)* Then, of course, they inevitably have to come back to me and ask for some fat size because they're fat.

JOE. Did you used to be fat or something?

KATIE. Excuse me?

JOE. You just keep harping on it.

KATIE. I was never fat!

JOE. I used to be fat.

KATIE. Okay.

JOE. I'm just saying …

KATIE. Well, great! Congratulations!

JOE. Anyway. *(DING DONG! The doorbell of the suite rings. Joe and Katie freeze. There is a moment without dialogue where Katie crawls underneath some furniture and Joe follows her on all fours. DING DONG! The doorbell rings again.)*

KATIE. *(Whispers.)* Open the door.

JOE. No way.

KATIE. *(Whispers.)* Oh my god. It's Pigface. It's so Pigface. We are so fucked.

JOE. Who?

KATIE. Please open the door.

JOE. I don't know who it is.

KATIE. Neither do I.

JOE. So … Fuck! I left my bowl over there. *(DING DONG! Another ring.)*

KATIE. *(Screams.)* It's the fucking cops! Oh my god!

JOE. Shh! *(Joe wrestles her to the ground and puts his hand over Katie's mouth just as … Jeff reenters. He's not naked per se. But, you know, we get it.)*

JEFF. *(Shouts.)* Just a second! *(To himself.)* Fucking Christ. *(Jeff opens the door and exits. An offstage altercation. Joe strains to hear. Jeff reenters with a tray of coffee and sets it down somewhere. He picks up a cup for himself and notices Joe. Katie cannot see Jeff. Jeff stares at them. Then he smiles and gives Joe a "thumbs up." He picks up a cup for Regan and exits. Joe releases Katie. The entire ordeal has exhausted her. Neither of them move.)*

JOE. Sorry I did that to your mouth.

KATIE. I don't care.

JOE. *(Wipes his hand.)* You didn't have to keep licking it like that.

KATIE. That's how I would get my brothers to stop smothering me.
JOE. Right. Are you … just gonna be okay down here then?
KATIE. I don't feel like moving. *(He moves to go get the bowl. Katie stops him.)* Where are you going?
JOE. Nowhere.
KATIE. Stay down here.
JOE. But we're on the floor.
KATIE. I think it's romantic.
JOE. To be on the floor.
KATIE. Yeah.
JOE. But it's uncomfortable.
KATIE. No it's not. *(She goes to grab a champagne bottle. Joe stops her.)*
JOE. You're gonna choke if you drink that lying down.
KATIE. I'm fine!
JOE. Let's just go on the couch.
KATIE. Please kiss me.
JOE. But …
KATIE. Please … I really need it.
JOE. Katie. *(She kisses him. He kisses her back. Barely.)*
KATIE. Your facial hair is so weird. *(They kiss again. She grinds against his crotch. He tries to get into it but eventually he pulls away.)*
JOE. I really don't think we should do this.
KATIE. Do what?
JOE. Let's just drink some coffee and smoke some weed.
KATIE. Why don't you like me?
JOE. I do like you.
KATIE. Why don't you want to have sex with me?
JOE. I do.
KATIE. Then, let's do it.
JOE. I really don't want to right now, Katie.
KATIE. *(Getting upset.)* You think I'm not pretty.
JOE. You're beautiful. You're gorgeous.
KATIE. I'm so gross.
JOE. You're the most beautiful girl I've ever seen.
KATIE. Then PLEASE!
JOE. I want to sleep with you. But you're not okay right now.
KATIE. I'm FINE!
JOE. No you're not.
KATIE. Just kiss me again.
JOE. You taste like vomit. *(Mortified, Katie cries out in a very primal*

and unfeminine way. It's a howl of embarrassment and defeat. No woman has ever made this sound.)

KATIE. AAAAAAaaaggghh! *(She turns away from him and is silent. Joe touches her hair.)*

JOE. Katie …

KATIE. *(Flinches away.)* You're such a poser.

JOE. I'm what?

KATIE. You're just like the rest of them. You're a phony.

JOE. You have no reason to be mad at me.

KATIE. Oh really?

JOE. I've done nothing but try to help you since I met you an hour ago.

KATIE. Don't you get it, you stupid fucking phony?! THIS is what Marilyn Monroe looks like!! *(They stare at each other for a moment.)*

JOE. Do you want me to go?

KATIE. I stopped caring about you a while ago.

JOE. I don't get it. What am I supposed to do?

KATIE. Nothing.

JOE. But you just screamed at me —

KATIE. Just make me feel better.

JOE. I don't think I can do that.

KATIE. Please just make this like it was a couple of minutes ago.

JOE. I don't know how.

KATIE. Then get out of here.

JOE. Will that make you feel better?

KATIE. Fine. *(Joe gets his things and exits the suite without lingering. A prisoner being released. He leaves the door ajar. Katie cries. Not like a grown person but like a little girl whose toy is broken. She boxes her own ears. A harsh attempt to snap herself out of feeling. To herself, methodically.)* Stop it. Stop it. Stop it. You're worthless. You're worthless. You're worthless. Everyone hates you everyone hates you everyone hates you … *(She sees Regan's purse and rummages through it.)* Come on. Come on. *(She finds a pill bottle. A different one than Regan used earlier. A different color.)* Jack. Pot. *(Katie takes a handful of pills. She doesn't empty the bottle. She replaces the bottle in Regan's purse. She swallows the pills and washes them down with champagne. She chokes, then chugs again. Suddenly — Joe bursts back into the suite. He goes straight to Katie and kisses her deep and long. Movie star kisses her. I mean, sweeps her off of her feet.)*

37

JOE. Did that work? *(Katie stares at him.)* I've always wanted to do something like that. *(Katie sways back and forth for a moment. Then ...)*

KATIE. Joe?

JOE. Yeah?

KATIE. It's not working. *(Blackout.)*

Scene Three

Thirty minutes later.

The suite is empty but as it was. A disaster.

After a moment, Regan emerges from the bedroom. A bed sheet wrapped around her. She goes for the coffee and gulps a mug full. The coffee is ice cold so she instantly opens her mouth and coffee spills all over her chest.

REGAN. Shit. Fuck. *(Her cell phone catches her eye. She looks at it.)* Douchebag. *(She makes a call. Into the phone.)* What?! ... Why the fuck are you calling me a million times? ... It was on vibrate ... I'm at Becky's thing. I told you we would be out late ... You go out every fucking Saturday with your meathead friends and I go out once ... ONCE in the last six months and you give me shit for it ... Uh huh ... Yeah ... Well, I don't care ... because you're an idiot ... Yeah ... I TOLD you we'd be OUT late ... *(She sees Joe's bowl. She finds a lighter and takes a hit. Into the phone.)* You don't care anyway ... Your residency my ass-fuck-face ... No, I'm not smoking ... I'm NOT SMOKING ... I fucking quit three years ago ... for you ... and you don't trust me ... that's what this comes down to ... You ... you ... CAN I SAY SOMETHING?! *(Jeff enters from the bedroom. He's practically dressed. He picks up a coffee as well. He spits it back into the cup. Into the phone.)* Can I say one thing at this juncture before you start acting like ... LISTEN! If you can't trust me, then I don't know what the fucking point of me EVER leaving the house ... I'll just bake a casserole and then lie around with my

38

legs open until you feel like ... YOU ARE SUCH A BABY! ... That's stupid ... Well, I think you're stupid ... I'll be home when I feel like coming home ... FINE! MAYBE I WILL! *(She hangs up and tosses the cell phone away.)*

JEFF. Trouble in paradise?

REGAN. That was just ... you know ...

JEFF. Him?

REGAN. Yeah.

JEFF. Yep.

REGAN. I'm ... uh ... look. This is weird.

JEFF. Don't make it weird.

REGAN. Excuse me?

JEFF. It's never weird unless you make it weird.

REGAN. Unless *I*...?

JEFF. Yes. *(Regan works up the courage to say something.)*

REGAN. You really shouldn't have ...

JEFF. *(Reminiscing their tryst.)* I had to.

REGAN. You should've asked me first.

JEFF. Aw ... And take all the fun out of it?

REGAN. You're an asshole.

JEFF. Don't tell me that was the first time you ever had a guy ... *(Regan is silent.)* That's what I figured.

REGAN. You don't know anything about me.

JEFF. You say that like it's a bad thing.

REGAN. Whatever.

JEFF. Don't tell me you feel guilty?

REGAN. I don't!

JEFF. Good girl.

REGAN. I'm ... just tired. It's late. He just chewed me out.

JEFF. I'll make you a deal. I won't tell him if you won't.

REGAN. *(Pause.)* Why is it so quiet? *(Then ...)* KATIE?! *(Regan goes into the bathroom. Offstage.)* Oh for fuck's sake.

JEFF. What now?

REGAN. *(Offstage.)* Katie passed out and your stupid friend just left her here.

JEFF. Joe's a good guy. I'm sure he's around ... somewhere. She okay?

REGAN. *(Offstage.)* I knew she'd fall asleep. I TOLD her NOT to! *(Regan reenters and gets her cell phone. She dials. During the following, dialogue, her phone call keeps going to voicemail so she ends it and redials several times.)* You guys should probably go now.

39

JEFF. Wow.

REGAN. Wow what?

JEFF. Quite the emancipated woman over here. Use me for sex and then kick me to the curb?

REGAN. Shut up.

JEFF. I feel like I just scored myself a guest spot on *Sex and the City*.

REGAN. All you do is fucking talk.

JEFF. This is the episode where Carrie cheats on her boyfriend only to complain a season later about how men are the ones afraid of commitment.

REGAN. What is wrong with you?

JEFF. You don't really expect me to answer that, do you? *(There is a knock at the door. Jeff goes to answer it as Regan finally leaves a voice-mail message.)*

REGAN. *(Into the phone.)* Gena? Where are you? I just walked into the bathroom and Katie ... she's — Fucking call me back, okay? Shit got real. *(Joe enters. He holds Katie's purse.)*

JEFF. Nice purse.

JOE. It's Katie's. She asked me to go get it.

JEFF. Okay. Well, we've been asked to clear out.

JOE. What?

REGAN. Yeah, you guys should probably go soon.

JEFF. Charming AND polite.

JOE. I just need to check on Katie.

REGAN. I just did.

JOE. I just need to give her ... give her this. *(He exits to the bathroom.)*

REGAN. I cannot believe I got stuck with her tonight.

JEFF. She got pretty fucked up.

REGAN. She's ALWAYS like this. It's so annoying.

JEFF. I'm gonna go put my shoes on.

REGAN. No one's stopping you.

JEFF. Easy there, Miss "Hit the Road." Surely you won't deny me the proper footwear for a proper exit.

REGAN. Jeff.

JEFF. Yeah?

REGAN. What's my name? *(A silence. He laughs uncomfortably. He doesn't know.)* Just put your shoes on. *(Jeff exits to the bedroom. Joe reenters. Regan texts on her cell phone.)*

JOE. Um ... where's Jeff?

REGAN. In the bedroom. Leaving. Why?

JOE. Oh my god.

REGAN. What?

JOE. Katie. She won't wake up. I can't get her to wake up.

REGAN. She's a drunk.

JOE. No. This is bad. She's like really not moving or something.

REGAN. Or something? She's breathing …

JOE. I think so.

REGAN. She blacked out. I turned her on her side.

JOE. No. Man. This is bad. She's out. I shook her really hard.

REGAN. She's just fucked up.

JOE. I shook her HARD.

REGAN. I heard you the first time.

JOE. I'm really freaked out. We should call someone.

REGAN. Who?

JOE. Like an ambulance.

REGAN. Katie doesn't need an ambulance. We just throw water on her.

JOE. *(Severely.)* Dude.

REGAN. *(Just as severely.)* What?

JOE. Listen to me. She's not waking up. This is not good.

REGAN. Okay. I have known this girl since high school. She is ALWAYS like this. We just throw water on her. *(Jeff reenters.)*

JEFF. What's happening?

JOE. Katie's not waking up.

JEFF. Did she drink more?

JOE. Not that much more. I was with her the whole time.

JEFF. You weren't here a second ago.

JOE. Well, when I went to the car. I wasn't here when I went to the car.

JEFF. Was she okay before that?

JOE. She was, like, nodding off. I thought she was tired.

JEFF. Then she's probably doing this thing called "sleep."

JOE. No, man …

REGAN. I'm gonna get dressed. You guys figure it out. *(She exits to the bedroom.)*

JEFF. What's her name?

JOE. Katie.

JEFF. No the other one.

JOE. Um … Regan.

JEFF. Fuck!

JOE. Jeff …

JEFF. Right. Let's just see … if we can get her walking. Okay?

JOE. Okay. *(They exit to the bathroom. After a few moments … Becky enters the room. Holding a plate with a large piece of cake. She is indeed technically overweight but very pretty. This is due to the fact that she is dressed stylishly and expensively. Her jewelry is stunning, including a large diamond engagement ring. She carries herself with confidence and dignity.)*

BECKY. Regan? *(She takes in the suite. She surveys the mess. In a way, it does not surprise her.)* Regan? Are you here? *(Regan reenters, half-dressed.)*

REGAN. Yeah. *(Sees Becky.)* Becks!

BECKY. Oh. Are you fucking some —

REGAN. No! I was just … changing … back into my dress. I spilled some wine on it at dinner and …

BECKY. Right.

REGAN. You look great.

BECKY. Thanks, bitch.

REGAN. What's going on?

BECKY. I was just gonna ask you that …

REGAN. *(Gestures to the room.)* Just …

REGAN and BECKY. *(An inside joke.)* Heeeeeeeyyyyyyyyyyy!

BECKY. Well, that's what it's here for. The room. You know? Goin' crazy.

REGAN. I didn't really. I just knocked … over … some stuff.

BECKY. *(Suddenly mean.)* My stuff. You knocked over. My stuff.

REGAN. *(Recoiling.)* I'm sorry.

BECKY. *(Kind again.)* It doesn't matter. *(Re: presents.)* I was gonna return all that shit anyway.

REGAN. Yeah … Sweetie, what're you doing here?

BECKY. Cal decided he wants to spend tonight in separate rooms. Adorable, right? I can already tell Christmas with him is gonna be hilarious.

REGAN. Yeah.

BECKY. Is it gay that I'm excited for tomorrow?

REGAN. No. It's … I'm really happy for you, Becks.

BECKY. I totally get why people get married. It's like … Remember our first summer in New York. You and I.

REGAN. We were … out of our minds.

BECKY. Totes. Stayed out as late as we wanted because who fucking cared whether we came home. But now … God! It's weird but I'm, like, ready to come home. You know?

REGAN. Yeah … I do. It's just … So you're gonna stay here then?

BECKY. *(Suddenly mean again.)* It's my room.

REGAN. *(Instantly apologetic.)* Of course, Becks. Whatever you want.

BECKY. *(Kind again.)* Let's order room service and some scotch.

REGAN. I'd love to. But first there's something I have to —

BECKY. I don't care that you trashed the room, Regan. I'm just pissed you did it without me. It's my night. You know?

REGAN. Becks … *(BAM! There is a thud in the bathroom offstage.)* … I gotta talk to you.

BECKY. What was that?

REGAN. I know you didn't want anyone else here but … um … Katie …

BECKY. Oh my god.

REGAN. I know.

BECKY. Is she here?

REGAN. She was on this side of the park and gave me this whole guilt-trip about not being invited. And you know how she is.

BECKY. Where is she? *(Jeff and Joe enter, carrying Katie between them. Katie is out cold.)*

JEFF. Hey.

BECKY. Dear Lord.

REGAN. This is Jeff and Joe. Um … they're friends of Katie's.

BECKY. Yes. Yes they are.

JEFF. Are you the one who's getting married?

BECKY. *(Ruthless.)* What?

REGAN. They're gonna get rid of her now.

BECKY. I don't think they should "get rid of her." We can't just prop her up on a train to Greenport. I mean, fuck, can we? Is she okay?

JEFF. *(Relaxed.)* Oh yeah, I've seen this a thousand times. She just had an awesome night. That's all.

JOE. *(More concerned.)* We need to get her walking.

REGAN. I'm really sorry about this, Becks. I know you didn't want this kind of drama tonight.

BECKY. Is any of this coffee hot?

REGAN. It used to be.

BECKY. How long has she been like this?

JOE. Not long but —

BECKY. Maybe we should put her in the shower?

43

JEFF. It's full of champagne bottles.

BECKY. Of course you ordered champagne!

REGAN. No! They were there when I got here.

BECKY. *(Tickled.)* Cal must've done that. He's always doing stuff like that. Things he thinks Super-Cal would do. I fucking love him. Okay. Let's get those out of there and put her —

JEFF. I'm on it. *(Jeff leaves one side of Katie and exits to the bathroom. Joe cannot support her so Becky grabs Katie's other arm to keep her upright. Katie's head lolls onto Becky's shoulder. Vomit oozes out of Katie's mouth onto Becky's dress.)*

BECKY. Ah! Son of a whore!

REGAN. Oh shit. *(Regan grabs a napkin from the coffee tray. She wipes up the vomit.)*

BECKY. Don't worry about it, Regan.

REGAN. Put her on the couch.

JOE. She'll choke if we lie her down.

REGAN. Don't be so dramatic. This isn't 1968.

JOE. What does that mean?

BECKY. He's right. She's barfing. We shouldn't lie her down. Barfing … is a good sign though.

JOE. *(To Becky.)* You're awesome. I'm freaking out.

BECKY. It's okay. Katie does this a lot. She's breathing and everything. We just need to get her to wake up so she can keep throwing up.

JOE. *(Down for whatever.)* Okay.

BECKY. *(A brilliant idea comes to her.)* Regan, you should call Gena. She lives in Brooklyn still doesn't she? Bushwick?

REGAN. Yeah … but —

JOE. Who?

BECKY. Gena. She can get Katie up. She's done it practically every weekend since high school.

JOE. Do you really think we should wait for someone to come all the way from Brooklyn?

BECKY. Honestly, Katie's always —

JOE. *(Overlapping.)* — always like this. I know. I heard.

BECKY. *(To Regan.)* Call Gena. Tell her to call a car. I'll pay for it.

REGAN. I already tried her. She's probably snorting away her unwanted pregnancy.

BECKY. *(Laughs, then serious …)* You shouldn't joke about that.

REGAN. *(Smiles.)* I know.

BECKY. It's so sad. You're awful.

REGAN. I know.

JOE. *(To Becky.)* I think I got her. If you want to … *(Becky releases Katie. Joe can't support her alone but makes a valiant effort.)*

BECKY. *(To Regan.)* Where's your phone?

REGAN. Somewhere. In here. *(The girls look for Regan's cell. Becky in earnest. Regan half-heartedly.)* I'm really sorry. I know you didn't want the circus tonight.

BECKY. You can't help it. They follow you around like dogs.

REGAN. Or little children.

BECKY. It's my fault. I should've bit the bullet and invited them.

REGAN. Nooooo!

BECKY. Yeaaaah. Then, at least, they might've behaved themselves.

REGAN. They couldn't even if they tried.

JEFF. *(Reenters.)* The tub is empty. We should take her clothes off.

BECKY. Here it is! *(Becky finds Regan's phone. She dials Gena. Jeff and Joe undress Katie.)*

REGAN. Becky, I already left her a message. Honestly, these guys seem … you know … capable. They're her friends. Let them handle it. *(A cell phone rings. The ringtone comes from outside the suite. Everyone listens for a moment. The ringtone moves closer. Then … Gena enters. She holds a garbage bag containing Becky's wedding dress. She also carries a plastic bag from a deli filled with two Red Bull energy drinks. There are bits of tissue paper in her nose. At first, Gena doesn't notice anyone else in the suite. She fumbles with her purse to find her cell phone. When she does and answers, she sees everyone. Gena and Becky share a tense immediate connection.)*

GENA. Hi.

BECKY. Hi. Haven't seen you since …

GENA. The thing. *(They end their call simultaneously.)*

BECKY. What're you doing here?

GENA. You called me. *(Re: Katie.)* What the fuck is this?

JEFF. Who are you?

GENA. Who the fuck are you?!

BECKY. *(To Regan.)* How did she know to come here?

JEFF. Are you the one getting married?

GENA. What the fuck IS this?

REGAN. Give me. The dress. Please. *(Gena gives the garbage bag to Regan. She charges over to Jeff and Joe.)*

BECKY. *(Re: garbage bag.)* What dress? Whose dress?

REGAN. Mine. Bridesmaid dress. Taken in last minute. *(Becky turns her attention to Gena who, at that moment, smacks Jeff hard in the face. He lets go of Katie.)*

JEFF. Ow!

BECKY. Gena!

JEFF. We were trying to get her walking.

REGAN. You don't need to fucking hit the guy. *(Gena tickles Joe, trying to get him to release Katie. Joe won't let go.)*

GENA. Get off of her!

JOE. I'm trying to help!

GENA. GET OFF OR I SWEAR TO GOD I WILL KILL YOU! I WILL TAKE A BOTTLE TO YOUR FACE MOTHERFUCKER!

JOE. Jesus. *(He reluctantly lets go of Katie. Gena supports her alone.)*

GENA. You touch me or her and I will bash your fucking skulls in! *(Gena, with surprising strength, lugs Katie over to the couch. Gena lies Katie down on her back.)*

BECKY. He was keeping her upright.

REGAN. They were gonna put her in the shower!

JOE. Please don't lie her on the couch like that! *(Joe moves to touch Katie. Gena turns a champagne bottle upside down and wields it like a baseball bat. It was not empty. Champagne pours out all over the floor. Everyone backs off.)*

GENA. You think I'm fucking JOKING, asshole?! *(Gestures to Katie.)* Why is she naked? Christ! What IS this? National Date-Rape Day?!

BECKY. Nobody's raping anybody. We are trying to help.

GENA. *(To Regan.)* Did you leave her with these guys?

REGAN. Calm down, Gena.

GENA. You can't leave Katie with guys!

BECKY. *(To Regan.)* You invited Gena, too?! I should've known you'd —

REGAN. *(To Becky.)* No! They guilt-tripped me.

JEFF. *(To Gena.)* Joe was taking care of her.

GENA. I'm sure he did just that.

JOE. Fuck! I was just —

GENA. Hey! John Mayer! Great story! Get some water.

JOE. Fine! *(Joe exits to the bathroom. Gena cracks open a Red Bull and chugs it.)*

BECKY. This is a nightmare.

JEFF. *(To Regan.)* Don't you work in a hospital? Do something! Blow in her mouth or ...

REGAN. I read them books.

GENA. Regan, I know we can't help the fact that Katie's gonna pull a Sylvia Plath on us every fucking time we go out but all I ask is that you don't break cardinal girl rule number one and leave her with some skeezebag. Just turn her over on her side and call me.

BECKY. We did!

REGAN. Gena, please wake her up.

JEFF. Joe's not a skeezebag. *(Joe reenters with a tumbler of water. Gena finishes her Red Bull in record time.)*

JOE. I was taking care of her and talking to her and she was fine and then … she just couldn't keep her eyes open and —

GENA. *(To Katie.)* KATIE! WE'RE LEAVING NOW!

JEFF. You guys got it from here right? *(Gena throws the empty can at Jeff. Gena props Katie up in a sitting position. To Joe.)* I think they've totally got it from here.

JOE. Just wait a minute, Jeff.

GENA. *(Screaming.)* KATIE! YOU GOTTA WAKE UP! WE'RE GONNA GO EAT BURGERS AND FRENCH FRIES AND MILKSHAKES! *(Gena pours the glass of water very slowly onto Katie's chest. She sings to her. She sings Katie's favorite song. Romantic and old school [e.g., "Don't Worry Baby" by The Beach Boys*]. This does nothing. Katie remains deadly still. This unnerves Gena.)*

JOE. Has this worked with her before?

GENA. *(To Joe.)* Yes. It's her favorite song. It always gets her up.

JEFF. She's not getting up.

GENA. I can see that. *(To Joe.)* Get some more water. *(Joe exits to bathroom. Without warning, Gena hits Katie hard across the face. Nothing from Katie.)* You stupid drunk! Wake up! *(To Regan.)* This is your fault!

BECKY. Hey! Regan is not her babysitter.

GENA. But I guess I am. That's why everyone's fucking calling me!

BECKY. Well, where were you all night? Trying to score coke?

GENA. No. Actually. I was saving your fucking —

REGAN. *(Ice cold.)* She was fixing your wedding dress. *(Becky snatches the garbage bag from Regan. She struggles to open it.)* She got coked up and ripped it. I tried to stop her.

BECKY. Why is it in a bodybag? *(Joe comes back in with the water.)*

GENA. I don't have time for this bullshit. *(Gena pours the water on*

Katie just like before. She sings to her again. This time, everyone sings along. Katie stays motionless. Gena is now scared.)

REGAN. Okay, we need to think clearly about this. The best thing to do is get her out of here. The hotel. The wedding guests. The police.

GENA. Something's wrong.

REGAN. Obviously. I just think it's best if this doesn't happen ... here.

BECKY. Then where? The lobby? What happens if she never wakes up?

JOE. Gena, we need to get her to the hospital.

GENA. What'd she take? What'd you all do tonight?

REGAN. She did coke with you.

GENA. I know! What else?

BECKY. Oh Jesus! You brought coke here. Of course.

JEFF. We smoked. Some pot.

GENA. And ...

JEFF. And ... she drank some champagne.

GENA. The doctors could give her something that could kill her —

BECKY. Does this mean we're calling an ambulance?

GENA. — Unless I can tell them exactly what these guys gave her. *(She looks at Jeff.)*

JEFF. *(Offended.)* I don't roll like that —

GENA. Regan?

REGAN. What?

JOE. Regan!

REGAN. What?!

JOE. If she took something, tell us so we can get her out of here.

JEFF. Truth be told, they're gonna stick a tube down her throat so it doesn't really matter what went down. It's all coming up.

GENA. This toolbag is amazing.

JEFF. *(To Joe.)* Fuck this! We can totally head out, bro. I've seen this a dozen times. It works itself out.

JOE. Really? 'Cause I've seen it where it doesn't. Can we call 911?

GENA. Yes. Help me put her clothes back on.

JOE. Jeff?

JEFF. Dude ... The police?

JOE. Please! *(Jeff dials 911. Gena and Joe dress Katie and collect their things.)*

REGAN. Becks, is the dress okay?

BECKY. *(Livid.)* I don't even want to look at it. It's been in the hands of a maniac!

REGAN. Gena promised me she would fix it.

GENA. *(To Becky.)* Katie's in serious fucking trouble. Okay?! I'm sorry that it's impinging on your "day" or whatever but —

BECKY. You have done a lot of thoughtless fucked up selfish things to me but ruining my wedding dress? That's low. Even for you, Gena.

JEFF. *(Cupping the receiver of the phone.)* What's the address here?

JOE. 700 Fifth Avenue.

BECKY. If you don't have any respect for yourself then I can't force you to. I stopped trying to help you a long time ago.

REGAN. I'm really sorry, Becks. I shouldn't have let them come.

BECKY. I didn't want them here because they destroy EVERY-THING.

GENA. Which is exactly why Regan invited us.

JEFF. They're gonna be here in fifteen minutes. Let's jet.

JOE. I'm gonna bring her downstairs, first. Jesus, Jeff.

JEFF. That crazy girl's gonna handle it.

JOE. You can't seriously be ditching me now! *(Gena grabs Regan's purse. Regan wrestles with her for it.)*

REGAN. Hey! That's my stuff. *(The purse strap breaks and several prescription pill bottle tumble out and onto the floor. Gena and Regan scramble for them.)*

JEFF. *(Re: bottles.)* Whoa!

GENA. Which one, Regan? Which one. *(Holds up bottles.)* Which one? Xanax. Codine. Vicodin. Which one, Regan?

BECKY. *(Re: Katie.)* Jesus, she just fucking killed herself.

JEFF. Man, we can't be here when the cops get here.

JOE. I'm not leaving her.

GENA. Which bottle is not as full as it was when you got here?

JEFF. I can't do it, bro. None of these bitches are worth it.

BECKY. What the fuck, Regan?

JOE. Jeff!

REGAN. *(To Becky.)* It's my medicine!

JEFF. If you wanna stay here, then you certainly don't need me. *(Jeff exits. Gena has gotten most of the pill bottles away from Regan. Joe goes to Katie, readies her to leave.)*

REGAN. I have prescriptions. I need them.

BECKY. *(To Gena.)* I ... had no idea.

GENA. Cancer patients, my ass!

REGAN. Stop it, Gena!

GENA. I'll flush them if you don't fucking tell me.

REGAN. Don't you dare! *(Regan wrests the pill bottles away from Gena. Regan carefully but frantically inspects each bottle.)*

GENA. Becky, she WANTED this to happen. She told us you wanted us here. Then proceeded to ruin everything.

REGAN. I'm not some sort of sociopath. I didn't plan this disaster.

GENA. Well, it certainly helps your case that the only person who could back me up is crapshoot over here *(Gestures to Katie.)* who is going to DIE if you don't tell me what she TOOK!

REGAN. Klonopin. *(Joe lifts up Katie to bring her downstairs. Suddenly and subtly … Katie puts her arms around Joe. Then she goes limp again.)*

JOE. Katie?

GENA. Is she awake?

JOE. She just touched me.

GENA. Put her down.

JOE. *(To Gena.)* I got it! *(Softly.)* Katie? *(Katie softly sings a few bars of the song Gena sang to revive her.)* I don't know if you can hear me but … can you … put your arms around me again?

KATIE. Mmmm … *(Katie very slowly puts her arms around his neck. Despite the fact that Katie is practically comatose, this is a very intimate moment for Joe. Everyone is still.)*

JOE. *(To Gena but without taking his gaze off of Katie.)* Let's go. *(Gena gathers up the rest of their things.)*

GENA. Ladies. I'd love to stay and play "pass the blame" but Zach Braff and I have an ambulance to catch. Call me when you grow a conscience. *(They exit. Regan and Becky stand silent for a moment. Then, Becky moves to the garbage bag and takes out her dress. She looks at it for a long time.)*

REGAN. Becky —

BECKY. Oh my god.

REGAN. … I can explain.

BECKY. *(Might throw up.)* Oh my god.

REGAN. Yeah. I —

BECKY. Shut. Up.

REGAN. Um … Okay. I get that this is a really messed-up situation but you don't have to freak out on me.

BECKY. How could you let that happen?

REGAN. Why are you telling me to shut up?

BECKY. Are you some sort of junkie or something that you don't even know your shit —

REGAN. NO!

BECKY. Then why would you do this?

REGAN. First of all, I didn't do anything to you. Second of all, you said I could have the room —

BECKY. Because I wanted to be nice.

REGAN. — so it's actually none of your business what I do in it. It was an accident. I fixed it.

BECKY. Gena fixed it.

REGAN. Whatever.

BECKY. This isn't fair.

REGAN. I know.

BECKY. It isn't.

REGAN. You're going to look fine. *(Pause, then scoffs, almost to herself.)* No one's going to be looking at the dress. *(Becky glares at her.)* You know what I mean. They'll be looking at your … face. How happy you are. All that … fucking … shit.

BECKY. What? Are you talking about?

REGAN. I'm tired. Isn't it like one in the morning?

BECKY. I'm getting married tomorrow!

REGAN. So go to bed.

BECKY. Fuck it.

REGAN. What?

BECKY. I thought when you wanted to be my maid of honor —

REGAN. I didn't *want* to do this.

BECKY. You said that if I asked anyone else you'd cut my tits off.

REGAN. That was obviously a joke.

BECKY. But I wanted you to do this.

REGAN. To plan everything and stand there next to you. In front of everyone like a —

BECKY. I could've asked someone else.

REGAN. Stop it, Becks!

BECKY. I just thought that — I don't know what I was thinking. I didn't know it was this bad. I thought we could still be friends.

REGAN. We are friends.

BECKY. No we're not.

REGAN. Becky, I'm your friend. Okay? I don't understand why you feel like we're not.

BECKY. Gena really looks out for Katie.

REGAN. They pressured me into letting them come here. I shouldn't've —

BECKY. She's gonna spend the whole night in the emergency room with her. And if Katie doesn't wake up. She's willing to be there for that.

REGAN. Katie's gonna be fine. *(Beat.)* Come on, Becks. Let's take a look at this dress. It can't be that bad.

BECKY. DON'T TOUCH IT!

REGAN. Look, Becks. I don't even need this from you. Okay? I don't have to even be there tomorrow. *(Regan storms into the bedroom. Becky picks up Regan's pill bottles. Offstage.)* I really don't appreciate this shit from you. You know I get this kind of manipulative crap from Frank all day. If you're gonna act like this, then I'm leaving. *(Reenters.)* What are you doing?

BECKY. Are you expecting me to stop you from leaving or something?

REGAN. Excuse me?

BECKY. Honestly?

REGAN. Can you just … put those down so we can talk about it?

BECKY. Why?

REGAN. Please just put them down. *(Maliciously, Becky pretends to put down the bottles. Then, at the last moment, doesn't. She shakes her head.)* Do you know what people think when they look at you? Random people. People on the street. They are … what's the right word … what's the exact phrase … "grossed out." That's what they are. They're grossed out. And if you think that marrying Cal will fix that … it only *emphasizes* it.

BECKY. I can't control what people think.

REGAN. Oh, but you can, Becks. You just don't try hard enough. I've gotten so good at it that even a fat stupid pig thought I wanted to be her maid of honor. *(Becky coolly pours some pills into the palm of her hand.)* Stop.

BECKY. I get it.

REGAN. Give me those.

BECKY. I finally get you. *(Becky casually throws the pills so they scatter all over the room. Regan's hands turn into fists. Becky pours more pills out into her palm.)* Yep. *(Becky lets the pills slip through her fingers onto the floor. Regan tries not to move. Becky pours out more pills and scatters them. She dumps the remaining bottles onto* the floor. Regan shakes with anger. Beat.) You have to pick them up. Don't you?

REGAN. No, I don't.

BECKY. Yes, you do. Go on. Pick them all up and put them back in their little bottles. Prove my point.

REGAN. Fuck you, cunt.

BECKY. Weren't you just storming out of here a second ago? *(Opens the main door.)* Go on. Go on, Regan. Scot-free! *(Regan doesn't move. Becky stomps on a bunch of pills, crushing them.)*

REGAN. No! *(Regan rushes to the crushed pills and maniacally tries to pick their remains up. Becky watches this with the look of a woman who learned evil from the best. Regan tries to pick up the rest of the pills. She is desperate and frustrated. She whips herself into a frenzy until she stops and lets out a moaning sob. Then ... the two girls sit. Regan, on the floor, dejected. Becky, in a chair, stoic. Then ...)*

BECKY. You look great.

REGAN. Thank you. *(Blackout.)*

End of Play

PROPERTY LIST

Floral arrangements
White-wrapped wedding gifts
Cigarette, lighter
Bottles of expensive champagne
Ashtray
Purse with phone, prescription drug bottles, pills
Bag of coke, razor blade, rolled-up bill
Wedding dress
Glass vase
Cell phones
Regular phone
Bag of weed and bowl
Tray of coffee, cups, napkins
White bedsheet
Purse
Plate of cake
Large diamond engagement ring
Garbage bag with wedding dress
Plastic bag with two cans of Red Bull
Glass of water

SOUND EFFECTS

Doorbell
Cell phone ring, off

NOTES
(Use this space to make notes for your production)

NOTES
(Use this space to make notes for your production)